CONTENTS

KU-328-777

CHAPTER 1
LIGHTS, CAMERA,
ACTION!............... 4

CHAPTER 2
LAYING THE
FOUNDATION...... 6

CHAPTER 3
MAKING MOVES 10

CHAPTER 4
A NEW DIRECTION.......14

CHAPTER 5
NON-STOP ACTION.... 20

CHAPTER 6
WHAT'S NEXT FOR
DWAYNE ? 26

GLOSSARY............30
FIND OUT MORE....... 31
IINDEX 32

Lights, Camera, action!

To wrestling fans, he's "The Rock". To film buffs, he's simply Dwayne Johnson. He's a superstar who conquered the wrestling ring and is breaking the box office.

Towering at 2 metres (6 feet 5 inches) tall, Dwayne is a larger-than-life presence in more ways than one. His strong build and natural charm have helped him to become a huge star and an in-demand action hero. The *Hollywood Reporter* once said he had the "wit of Willis, the strength of Schwarzenegger, and the heart of Stallone". To date, Dwayne's films have pulled in a total of $3.7 billion (£2.6 billion).

This star's personality and entertaining antics can drive crowds crazy. And he doesn't plan on stopping any time soon. "What do I want?" Dwayne has said. "I want the world."

EDGE
BOOKS

HOLLYWOOD
ACTION HEROES

DWAYNE
JOHNSON

BY JEN JONES

Raintree is an imprint of Capstone Global Library Limited, a company incorporated in
England and Wales having its registered office at 264 Banbury Road, Oxford, OX2 7DY –
Registered company number: 6695582

www.raintree.co.uk
myorders@raintree.co.uk

ISBN 978 1 4747 2337 4
20 19 18 17 16
10 9 8 7 6 5 4 3 2 1

British Library Cataloguing in Publication Data
A full catalogue record for this book is available from the British Library.

Editorial Credits
Linda Staniford, editor; Kyle Grenz, designer;
Eric Gohl, media researcher; Gene Bentdahl, production specialist

Photo Credits
Alamy: AF Archive, 15, Moviestore Collection Ltd, 17, 25, Photos 12, 21; AP Photo: WWE/
Jonathan Bachman, 29; Getty Images: Collegiate Images, 9, George Pimentel, 10, Russell
Turiak, 13; Newscom: Album/John Bramley/Visual Arts Enter/Original Film/Columbia
Pictures Industries, 18-19, Album/Original Film, 22–23, Album/Paramount Pictures, 5,
Hutchins Photo/Kathy Hutchins, 7, iPhoto Inc./Greg Henkenhaf, 12; Shutterstock: Helga
Esteb, 26, 27, Tinseltown, cover, 1

Design Elements: Shutterstock

Dwayne as Roadblock in *G.I. Joe*

Laying the foundation

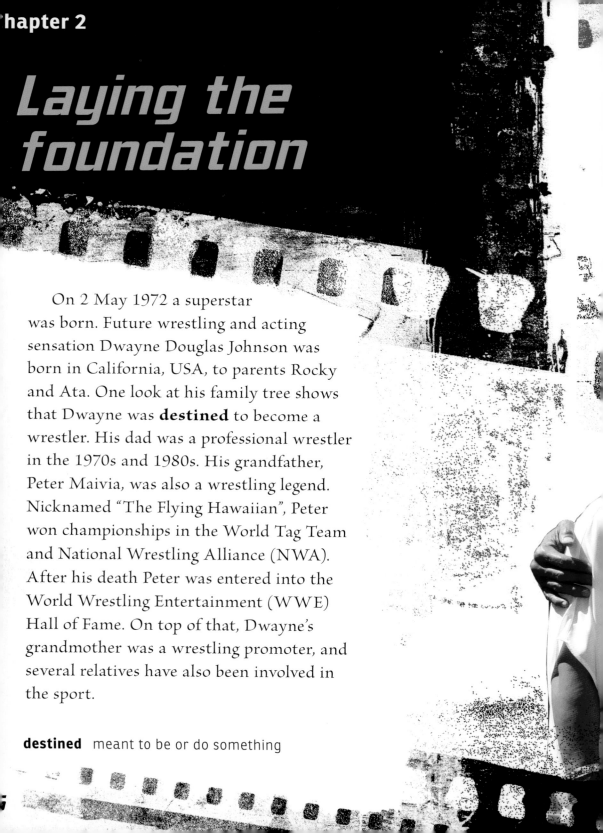

On 2 May 1972 a superstar was born. Future wrestling and acting sensation Dwayne Douglas Johnson was born in California, USA, to parents Rocky and Ata. One look at his family tree shows that Dwayne was **destined** to become a wrestler. His dad was a professional wrestler in the 1970s and 1980s. His grandfather, Peter Maivia, was also a wrestling legend. Nicknamed "The Flying Hawaiian", Peter won championships in the World Tag Team and National Wrestling Alliance (NWA). After his death Peter was entered into the World Wrestling Entertainment (WWE) Hall of Fame. On top of that, Dwayne's grandmother was a wrestling promoter, and several relatives have also been involved in the sport.

destined   meant to be or do something

Some of Dwayne's earliest memories include going to wrestling shows with his mum. His dad performed tricks such as flying off the top rope of the ring. Dwayne was so inspired that he often practised dropkicks in the living room. Later in life, these moves would come in handy – as Dwayne became one of wrestling's biggest stars of all time.

Dwayne's parents, Ata (left) and Rocky (right), have always been very supportive of his career.

Fast fact

Dwayne "The Rock" Johnson was the World Wrestling Federation's (WWF's) first third-generation wrestler.

Football prowess

Long before Dwayne became a wrestler, he was an American football player. When he was 16, his family moved to Pennsylvania. Dwayne's American football career started at Freedom High School. He was ranked as one of Pennsylvania's top eight players. Dwayne was also named in *USA Today*'s All-American team.

After graduating from high school in 1990, Dwayne earned a full football scholarship to the University of Miami in Florida. In 1991 he helped lead the Hurricanes, the university's team, to a national championship. However, a back injury during Dwayne's final year sidelined his dreams of playing in the National Football League (NFL). Dwayne did later join the Calgary Stampeders in the Canadian Football League (CFL). To his disappointment, he was dropped from the team just two months later. It was time to hang up the football shirt and see what else life held in store.

Dwayne wore the #94 shirt for the University of Miami Hurricanes.

In 1995, with just $7 (£5) to his name, Dwayne moved to Florida to be near his parents. Hoping to find a new career path, Dwayne asked his dad to teach him all about wrestling. Little did Dwayne know that he'd soon become a major force in the wrestling world.

Chapter 3

Making moves

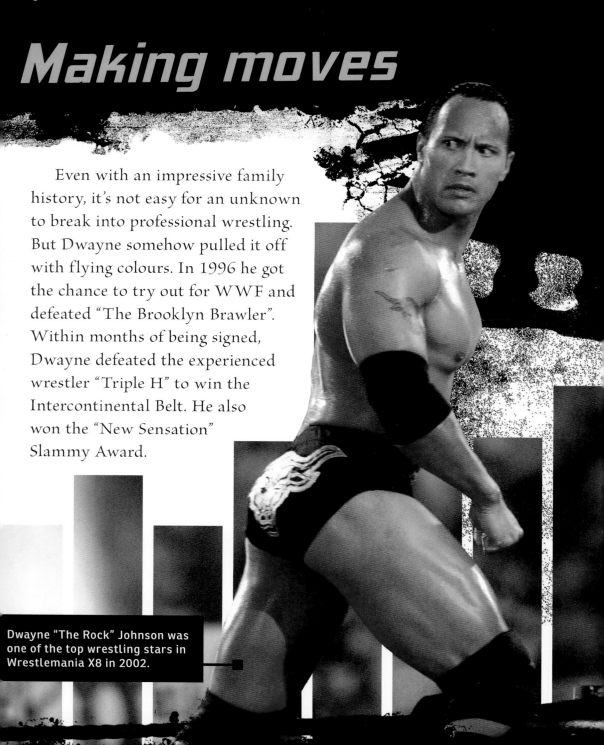

Even with an impressive family history, it's not easy for an unknown to break into professional wrestling. But Dwayne somehow pulled it off with flying colours. In 1996 he got the chance to try out for WWF and defeated "The Brooklyn Brawler". Within months of being signed, Dwayne defeated the experienced wrestler "Triple H" to win the Intercontinental Belt. He also won the "New Sensation" Slammy Award.

Dwayne "The Rock" Johnson was one of the top wrestling stars in Wrestlemania X8 in 2002.

Meet "The Rock"

All of these achievements happened for Dwayne in just over a year after his American football career ended. But as his success climbed, audiences began booing him. Fans in the 1990s wanted over-the-top "villains". Dwayne's nice guy image just wasn't working. It was time for a new approach. What emerged was "The Rock" – a tough-as-nails, tattooed bad boy in black boots. This **persona** would push him into the spotlight and mark the start of his **blockbuster** career.

persona a character or personality

blockbuster something that is very effective, successful, expensive, large or extravagant

Fast fact

Dwayne went by the names "Flex Kavana" and "Rocky Maivia" before settling on his famous nickname, "The Rock".

The *people's* champion

Reinvented as "The Rock", it didn't take long for Dwayne to reach the top of the wrestling heap. Dwayne was part of wrestling's "Attitude Era", where **trash-talking** and shock value were the name of the game. Fans went crazy for "The Rock's" catchphrases. Two favourites were: "Can you smell what 'The Rock' is cooking?" and "Know your role, and shut your mouth!"

trash-talking boastful way of talking used to threaten opponents

Dwyane wrestles Christian Cage at the Raw is War event in Toronto, Canada, 2001

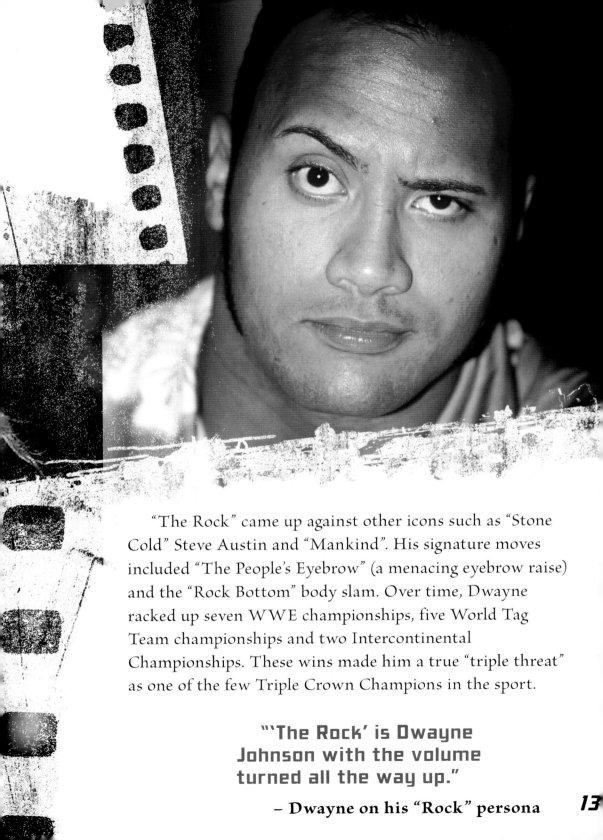

"The Rock" came up against other icons such as "Stone Cold" Steve Austin and "Mankind". His signature moves included "The People's Eyebrow" (a menacing eyebrow raise) and the "Rock Bottom" body slam. Over time, Dwayne racked up seven WWE championships, five World Tag Team championships and two Intercontinental Championships. These wins made him a true "triple threat" as one of the few Triple Crown Champions in the sport.

"'The Rock' is Dwayne Johnson with the volume turned all the way up."

– Dwayne on his "Rock" persona

13

Chapter 4

A new direction

Once "The Rock" became a household name, Hollywood began to take notice. His popularity led to invitations to be in a Wyclef Jean music video and on the TV series *Star Trek: Voyager*. Dwayne even played his own father, Rocky Johnson, on *That '70s Show*. He also appeared in several TV films, playing himself as "The Rock".

The doors to stardom were really thrown open for Dwayne when he hosted *Saturday Night Live* in 2000. Cracking jokes with Jimmy Fallon and Tina Fey, Dwayne proved he could command attention off the mat. After that night, his phone started ringing with offers from film studios. Like superstar Hulk Hogan before him, "The Rock" was set to dominate once again – this time as an actor.

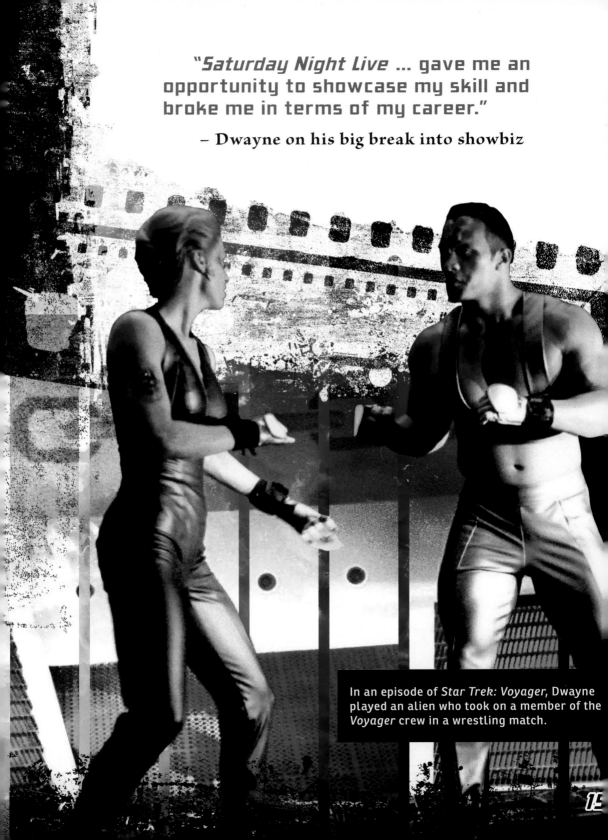

"*Saturday Night Live* ... gave me an opportunity to showcase my skill and broke me in terms of my career."

– Dwayne on his big break into showbiz

In an episode of *Star Trek: Voyager*, Dwayne played an alien who took on a member of the *Voyager* crew in a wrestling match.

15

It's good
to be king

In 2001 Dwayne landed his first film role in
The Mummy Returns. His powerful performance earned
him a Teen Choice Award.

Dwayne's success in his first film led to an exciting
offer to be the lead actor in the **prequel**, *The Scorpion
King* (2002). Dwayne played a fierce desert warrior.
The warrior's mission is to stop an evil king from
wiping out his homeland and its people. Filled with
fights and swordplay, the action-packed film was the
perfect way for "The Rock" to make the leap to films.

prequel story about events that happen to characters
before they appear in an existing story

Fast fact

In the final battle scene of *The Scorpion King*,
things got a little too heated. While fighting co-star
Steven Brand with flaming swords, Dwayne almost
burned his eyebrows off! The scene also featured
one of Dwayne's trusty wrestling moves, a "kip-up".
From lying down on the ground, he flips his body to
standing up using his legs and core strength.

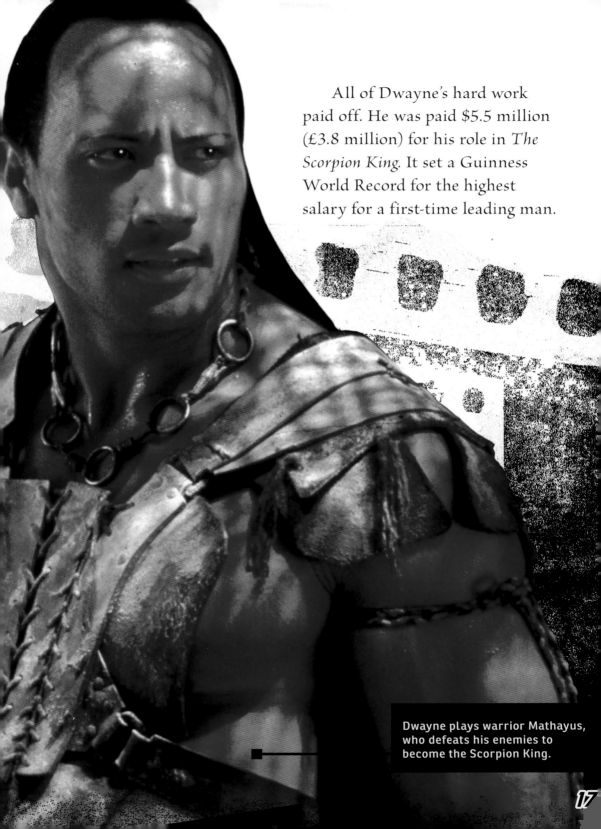

All of Dwayne's hard work paid off. He was paid $5.5 million (£3.8 million) for his role in *The Scorpion King*. It set a Guinness World Record for the highest salary for a first-time leading man.

Dwayne plays warrior Mathayus, who defeats his enemies to become the Scorpion King.

Worlds colliding

Dwayne's film roles gave him the chance to revisit his passion for American football.

In **Gridiron** *Gang* (2006), Dwayne plays Sean Porter. His character helps troubled youngsters by forming an American football team at a juvenile detention centre. The film was based on a true story. It was shot at the same place it was inspired by, Camp Kilpatrick in California, USA.

gridiron American football field with evenly spaced lines

Sport gives the kids in *Gridiron Gang* a new hope for the future.

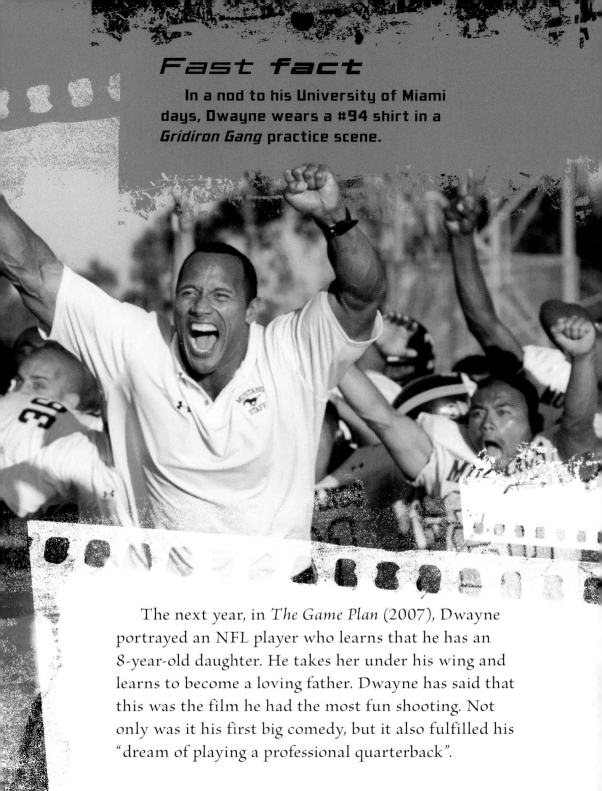

Fast fact

In a nod to his University of Miami days, Dwayne wears a #94 shirt in a *Gridiron Gang* practice scene.

The next year, in *The Game Plan* (2007), Dwayne portrayed an NFL player who learns that he has an 8-year-old daughter. He takes her under his wing and learns to become a loving father. Dwayne has said that this was the film he had the most fun shooting. Not only was it his first big comedy, but it also fulfilled his "dream of playing a professional quarterback".

Chapter 5

Non-stop action

What better way to get respect as an action star than to play some of history's most famous heroes? With *G.I. Joe: Retaliation* (2013) and *Hercules* (2014), Dwayne did just that.

Dwayne brought to life a tough-as-nails character called Roadblock in *G.I. Joe: Retaliation*. As the team's heavy machine gunner, Dwayne threw himself into the role. His elbows bled as he crawled through the desert during stunt scenes.

Playing Greek **demi-god** Hercules was also no easy feat. To build up his body for the role, Dwayne went on a 22-week power diet. He ate up to seven full meals a day with high-protein foods such as steak, egg whites, fish and broccoli. He even joked that he would drink "one cup of lion blood" every morning.

demi-god mythological being who is partly human and partly divine

To bulk up Dwayne also did heavy physical training. He worked out six days a week for six months. Once filming wrapped, Dwayne was proud of his hard work: "We've put a lot of blood, sweat, and tears into this movie."

"I had a massive collection of *G.I. Joe* and *Star Wars* action figures, and because I was an only child, they were my family and my friends."

– Dwayne on action heroes

Dwayne plays Roadblock, one of the *G.I. Joe* team that defeats terrorist organization COBRA in the film.

Life in the fast lane

The *Fast & Furious* series has always attracted an army of loyal fans. But when Dwayne came on board for the fifth film, *Fast Five* (2011), it gave the series a jolt of new life. On the opening weekend the film earned $86.2 million (£60 million), setting records for both Dwayne's films and the *Fast* **franchise**.

franchise series of films or TV programmes that feature the same characters or follow a continuing storyline

Dwayne can thank social media for the career-changing opportunity. His role was meant to go to an older actor. However, a fan's comment about wanting to see Vin Diesel take on "The Rock" changed everything. Enter DSS special agent Luke Hobbs, who drives a 10-tonne, **armoured** Gurkha truck. Director Justin Lin said that next to Dwayne, "anything less would look silly, like a clown car".

Fast Five's huge success led to Dwayne's return for the sixth and seventh *Fast & Furious* films. Now he's part of what Vin Diesel calls the "family of misfits".

armoured covered with metal to protect against attacks

Dwayne plays Luke Hobbs, a Security Service agent who is trying to bring down a group of criminals.

Shaking things up

Imagine an earthquake strong enough to break California, USA, in half. That's the plot of 2015's *San Andreas*, in which Dwayne plays a helicopter rescue pilot.

From the very first shot, Dwayne is in amped-up action hero mode. The opening scene features a woman whose car is teetering off the edge of a cliff. Dwayne's character must swoop in and save her, and not with fancy special effects. Instead, he had to dangle 46 metres (150 feet) out of a helicopter to do so. The director wanted the actors to do their own stunts so the audience could see their faces. "This isn't a trick. There's no editing," he said. "This is Dwayne really doing it."

That's not to say there were no special effects in the film. More than 1,300 special effects were shot in the air, underground and underwater. Dwayne filmed many scenes in a giant tank filled with more than 9 million litres (2 million gallons) of water. It's all in a day's work for this action hero!

In *San Andreas* Dwayne plays helicopter rescue pilot Ray Gaines.

What's next for Dwayne?

Dwayne devotes much of his time to good causes, especially those that help children in need. His Dwayne Johnson Rock Foundation works to help sick or disadvantaged young people. On the 2014 reality TV programme *Wake-Up Call*, Dwayne mentored a group of adult "everyday heroes". He helped them to rise above various challenges, and even helped to save a failing business.

Dwayne adds his handprints to those of many other Hollywood stars at the Forecourt of the Stars on Hollywood Boulevard in 2015.

THEATRE IMAX

When not saving the world or making films, Dwayne's got plenty of hobbies to keep him busy. He can often be found fishing. Early in 2015, he even caught a 91-kilogram (200-pound) fish called a tarpon! Dwayne also likes to show off his silly side. In 2014 he surprised crowds at a Hollywood comedy club with a hilarious stand-up routine. There's rarely a dull moment when "The Rock" is around!

Rock solid

In 2013 Dwayne's films were the highest **grossing** films in the world, bringing in $1.3 billion (£0.9 billion). Dwayne continues to make films, but he has also returned to the wrestling ring for special events. In WrestleMania 29 in 2013, his **bout** with John Cena attracted more than 80,000 WWE fans to the MetLife Stadium in New Jersey, USA. In 2014 he joined forces with Hulk Hogan and "Stone Cold" Steve Austin to kick off WrestleMania 30.

Dwayne Johnson's star power isn't going to dim any time soon. He always seems to have a new move up his sleeve. Wrestling star or action film hero, his fans are eager to see what he will do next.

grossing earning or bringing in money

bout contest or trial of strength, such as a wrestling or boxing match

Fast fact

"The Rock" is huge on social media, too. He has tens of millions of followers. In May 2015, he broke a world record by taking 105 selfies in three minutes!

"I want to do more in the [WWE]. I want to do more in the movie industry. Ultimately, I want to be the most electrifying man in sports entertainment."

– Dwayne on his future career

JUST
BRING
IT

Dwayne appears regularly at Wrestlemania. Here he is at the 2014 event, wearing a shirt with his slogan "Just Bring It".

GLOSSARY

armoured covered with metal to protect against attacks

blockbuster something that is very effective, successful, expensive, large or extravagant

bout contest or trial of strength, such as a wrestling or boxing match

demi-god mythological being who is partly human and partly divine

destined meant to be or do something

franchise series of films or TV programmes that feature the same characters or follow a continuing storyline

gridiron American football field marked with evenly spaced lines

grossing earning or bringing in money

persona character or personality

prequel story about events that happen to characters before they appear in an existing story

trash-talking boastful way of talking used to intimidate opponents

FIND OUT MORE

BOOKS

Dwayne "The Rock" Johnson (Modern Role Models), James A Corrick (Mason Crest, 2013)

The Art and Making of Hercules, Brett Ratner and Linda Sunshine (HarperCollins Publishers, 2014)

WWE Ultimate Superstar Guide, Steve Pantaleo (DK/BradyGames, 2015)

WEBSITES

www.dogomovies.com/category/action

Read children's reviews of action films.

www.kidzworld.com/article/28178-dwayne-johnson-the-rock-bio

Find out more about Dwayne's life.

mattel.wwekids.com

Play wrestling games.

INDEX

American football 8, 18
    scholarship to University of
      Miami 8

Canadian Football League (CFL) 8
charity work 26

Fast Five (2011) 22
Fast & Furious series 22–23

Game Plan, The (2007) 19
G.I. Joe: Retaliation (2013) 20
Gridiron Gang (2006) 18

Hercules (2014) 20
hobbies 27

Johnson, Ata (mother) 6
Johnson, Rocky (father) 6, 14

Maivia, Peter (grandfather) 6
Mummy Returns, The (2001) 16

San Andreas (2015) 24–25
Saturday Night Live (TV series) 14
Scorpion King, The (2002) 16, 17
Star Trek: Voyager (TV series) 14

That '70s Show (TV series) 14
"The Rock" 4, 11, 12, 14, 23

Wake-Up Call (TV series) 26
WrestleMania 28
wrestling 4, 6, 7, 9, 10, 12, 13, 16, 28
    awards 10
    championships 13
    image 11
    moves 13, 16
    special events 28